D0548931

WORLD ORGANIZATIONS

Amnesty International

FRANKLIN WATTS
A Division of Grolier Publishing
NEW YORK • LONDON • HONG KONG • SYDNEY
DANBURY, CONNECTICUT

Acknowledgments:
Picture credits:
Cover: Popperfoto (both)
Inside: Amnesty International: pp.3(bottom), 4, 6 (top), 9, 10(top), 11(left), 13(top), 14(both), 15, 16(left), 19(bottom), 21(bottom), 25, 26(top), 27(bottom). Popperfoto: pp. 2(both), 5(both), 6(bottom), 7, 8, 13(bottom), 17, 18, 19(top), 20(bottom), 23(both), 24, 25(top), 26(bottom), 27(top), 28, 29.
Topham: p.3(top), 5, 10, 11(right), 12, 13(top), 22.

Series editor: Sarah Snashall
Designer: Simon Borrough
Picture research: Sue Mennell
Consultant: Amnesty International UK

Visit Franklin Watts on the internet at:
http://publishing.grolier.com

First published in 2000 by Franklin Watts

First American edition 2001 by Franklin Watts
A Division of Grolier Publishing
90 Sherman Turnpike, Danbury, CT 06816

This title was produced with Amnesty International's advice, but the views expressed within do not necessarily reflect the views of Amnesty International.

Cataloging-in-Publication Data is available from the Library of Congress

ISBN 0-531-14619-7 (library bdg.)
0-531-14811-4 (pbk.)

Printed in Malaysia

Contents

1. Working for Human Rights

Amnesty International is a worldwide organization that tries to help people who are being held in prison because of their political or religious beliefs. It also works to end the use of torture and other kinds of cruel treatment of prisoners.

Human Rights

Amnesty International bases its work on the Universal Declaration of Human Rights, a list of rights for all people, proclaimed by the United Nations in 1948.

Checklist

The Universal Declaration of Human Rights states that:

- everyone has the right to life, liberty, and security of person
- everyone has the right to freedom of thought, conscience, and religion
- everyone has the right to freedom of opinion and expression
- no one shall be tortured, treated, or punished in a way that is cruel, inhuman

▲ *Amnesty International's symbol is a burning candle (representing hope) encircled by barbed wire (representing imprisonment).*

Prisoners of Conscience

However, thousands of people are still denied these basic rights. Worldwide, thousands of people are in prison without having committed any crime. They have been arrested because they have political or religious beliefs different from their governments'. Many have been arrested for exercising their freedom of expression — for saying or writing things that the government disliked. These people are called 'prisoners of conscience'. Amnesty International works to obtain the release of prisoners of conscience.

Journalists in France protest on behalf of imprisoned Iranian writer Faraj Sarkouhi.

Spotlight

Faraj Sarkouhi was imprisoned for writing magazine articles that criticized the Iranian government. Amnesty International adopted him as a prisoner of conscience. After his release, Sarkouhi explained how important Amnesty International's support was for people in Iran, where the individual "feels small, powerless, and utterly defenseless." He said: "If one learns that there is an organization like Amnesty International ... it gives you new strength."...

▸ *Hanging someone by the arms is a form of torture. Amnesty International campaigns against all forms of torture.*

Paul Deekor, who was imprisoned in Nigeria for protesting the damage caused by oil companies.

Political Prisoners

Amnesty International also concerns itself with the fate of political prisoners. These are people who have broken the law — in some cases using violence — because they are in political conflict with their government. Amnesty International does not demand the release of political prisoners, but it does demand that they receive a fair trial — many are jailed without any trial at all. It also tries to prevent them from being mistreated in prison.

Spotlight

In June 1989, Liu Xin, a 15-year-old boy living in China, went out into the street to watch a demonstration by people wanting freedom and democracy. As he stood there, he was arrested by the Chinese police. They alleged that he had given a match to a protester who used it to start a fire. For this crime — which he denied committing — Liu was sentenced to 15 years in prison. He was still behind bars in 1999.

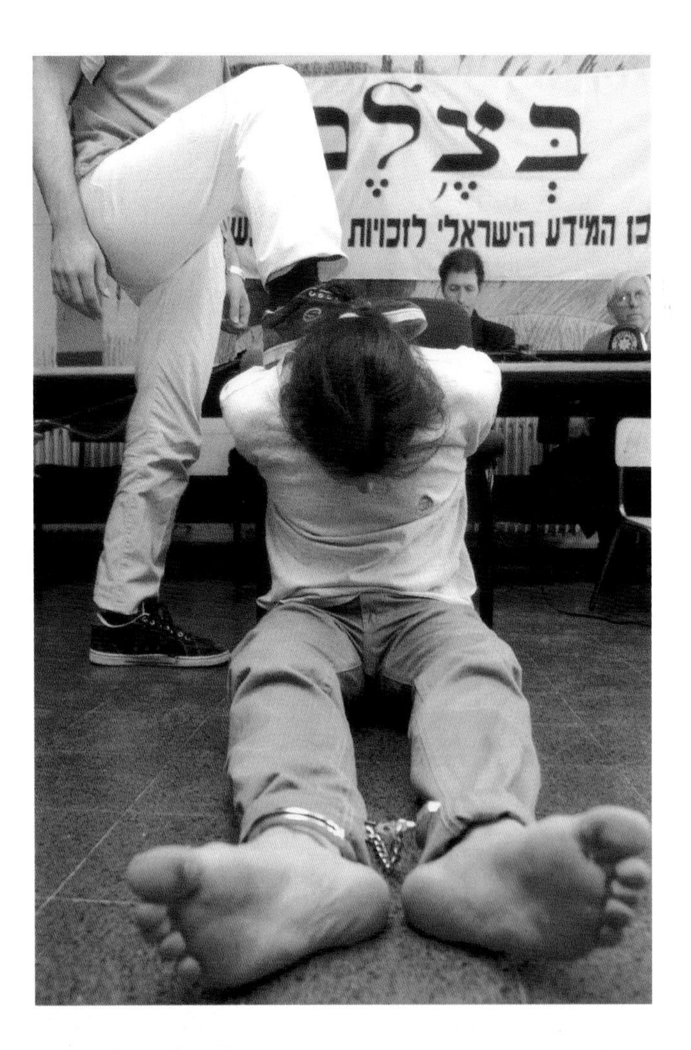

Torture

Both prisoners of conscience and political prisoners are often the victims of mistreatment. Torture is used in many countries every day. Prisoners are beaten, burned, given electric shocks, dosed with harmful drugs, or subjected to mock executions.

An Israeli human rights group demonstrates how prisoners are tortured by Israel's secret service.

Sometimes prisoners are tortured to obtain information, but often they are tortured simply as an extra punishment. This is a way of terrorizing people opposed to the government and discouraging them from speaking out.

Cruel Treatment

Amnesty International also opposes any "cruel, inhuman, or degrading treatment," such as locking prisoners up in the dark or chaining them with handcuffs. Such cruel treatment may lead to prisoners suffering mental and physical breakdowns or to dying.

Spotlight

Steve Biko (right) was one of the leaders of black resistance to white rule in South Africa in the 1970s. In September 1977, Biko was arrested by South African police. He was kept naked in handcuffs and leg irons, and severely beaten until eventually he died of head injuries. He was 30 years old.

Problem

Amnesty International campaigns against the use of capital punishment – execution – under all circumstances, even when the person concerned has been found guilty of murder after a fair trial. This view is controversial, especially in the United States, where a majority of people support the death penalty and more than 1,000 executions have taken place in the last 20 years. Amnesty International insists that execution, however terrible the person's crime, violates that person's right to life.

▸ A protest by relatives of people who "disappeared" in Chile during the dictatorship of General Augusto Pinochet.

Capital Punishment

Death is the ultimate punishment. About 90 countries have the death penalty — the legal right to execute people who have committed serious crimes. Some countries also practice "extrajudicial murder" — killing prisoners without any trial or other legal process. These killings may take place in secrecy, so that large numbers of men, women, and children simply "disappear" after being arrested.

Amnesty International not only opposes extrajudicial murder and "disappearances," but it also campaigns against any use of the death penalty, even for murderers.

Opposition Abuses

Not all crimes against humanity are committed by governments. Amnesty International has investigated and protested similar actions by guerrillas and opposition groups — hostage-taking, executions, and torture. It has, for example, sent a team of people to Northern Ireland to investigate "punishment beatings," used by armed groups such as the IRA as a form of primitive "criminal justice."

Pressure for Change

Amnesty International works by mobilizing public opinion. Governments want wrongful imprisonment, torture, and other abuses to remain secret. Amnesty International brings wrong-doing into the spotlight. By investigating and publicizing such cases, it creates pressure on governments to change their ways and respect human rights.

Spotlight

In 1976, a military government took power in Argentina. They waged what was called the "dirty war" against their opponents in the country. During this time, more than 30,000 people "disappeared" – they had been taken away by the police or army and secretly murdered. Relatives of those who disappeared are still struggling to find out the whole truth about what happened to their loved ones.

Checklist

Amnesty International:

- works to obtain release for prisoners of conscience
- works to obtain fair trials for political prisoners
- opposes cruel, inhuman, or degrading treatment for all prisoners
- opposes extrajudicial murder
- campaigns against the death penalty.

◀ Glen McGinnis, who is on death row for a crime he committed when he was 17. His mother was a drug addict, and he was abused by his stepfather.

2. An "Appeal for Amnesty"

From Britain–An 'Appeal for Amnesty, 1961'

PRISONERS BEHIND BARBED WIRE — A cartoon from "The Observer."

▲ *Benenson's 1961 newspaper article appealing for the release of prisoners of conscience.*

Today, Amnesty International is a large organization, but it grew from very small beginnings. In 1961, a British lawyer named Peter Benenson read about a group of students in Portugal who had been put in prison. All they had done was drink a toast to freedom.

Forgotten Prisoners

Benenson was appalled that people could be imprisoned so unjustly. He knew that worldwide there were thousands of other people in jail who had not committed crimes. He decided to launch an appeal in a newspaper on behalf of the "forgotten prisoners." The appeal called for the release of all people imprisoned because of their beliefs. It was Benenson who named them prisoners of conscience.

More than a thousand individuals contacted him — they too wanted to do something about these injustices. Amnesty International was formed by this network of volunteers. The name was chosen because "amnesty" means a general pardon and release from prison — though this does not precisely describe Amnesty International's work today.

▶ *British lawyer Peter Benenson, who started Amnesty International.*

Focusing on Individuals

Amnesty International volunteers wrote letters to the authorities in countries where prisoners of conscience were being held, calling for their release. The campaign quickly caught on. Many people liked Amnesty International's focus on individual prisoners. Volunteers who wrote letters calling for a prisoner's release felt they were becoming personally involved with the prisoner's fate.

At first, many people doubted that writing letters to brutal governments would work. But many prisoners were released, or saw their conditions improve, at least partly due to pressure from Amnesty International.

AMNESTY

Journal of the AMNESTY movement
An international movement for freedom of opinion and religion

No. 14 3rd January, 1962

1s. post free U.K.
1s. 3d. post free abroad

For subscriptions see page 7

F. Pizon
Prison Unknown
to Minister of Justice
Madrid
Espagne

DEVUELVASE AL REMITENTE POR ESTAR EN LIBERTAD EL DESTINATARIO

Hopeful news for AMNESTY arrived the other day on the front of this envelope. One of our supporters in Switzerland sent a Christmas card to a prisoner of conscience in Spain. It came back from the prison authorities marked RETURN TO SENDER AS THE CONSIGNEE IS FREE

▲ *Early evidence of success: A card sent by an Amnesty International member to a prisoner in Spain in 1962 has been returned saying he is no longer in jail.*

▼ *In 1967, an Amnesty International candle is lit by 14-year-old Michael Kyrkok. His father, a Greek politician, had been arrested after a military coup.*

Soviet Dissidents

Amnesty International was founded during the Cold War, when the United States and its allies were hostile to the communist Soviet Union. Some of Amnesty International's most prominent work was for dissidents in the Soviet Union — people who spoke out against communism. Amnesty International campaigned for the release of imprisoned dissidents.

A Reliable Reputation

Amnesty International gradually won a reputation for being an unbiased and reliable source of information about injustices and ill-treatment worldwide. To protect its independence, Amnesty International has never accepted money from governments, or political or religious groups.

◂ *Russian poetess Irina Ratushinskaya arrives in Britain with her husband after being released from prison in the Soviet Union in 1986. She had been arrested three years earlier.*

In 1977 Amnesty International was awarded the Nobel Peace Prize for its work. In the 1980s a number of musicians and artists supported Amnesty International as a special cause. They gave concerts and performances and donated the profits to Amnesty International. As a result, Amnesty International grew still more in size and in fame. New staffs were hired, and new offices were opened all over the world.

Problem

Amnesty International's work on behalf of the Soviet dissidents was especially popular in the United States, but was denounced by the Soviet Union. However, when Amnesty criticized the use of torture in South American countries backed by the United States, it was the Americans and their allies who were offended.

Spotlight

Amnesty International has been denounced by governments of many different kinds. In 1981, for example, the government of Guatemala described Amnesty International as a communist organization that "does not even try to hide its Soviet character." Around the same time, the Soviet Union said Amnesty International was an anti-communist tool of "imperialist security services" such as the American CIA.

Growing Influence

Amnesty International is now one of the most influential non-governmental organizations (NGOs) in the world. Its representatives are listened to with respect by the United Nations and many governments. Its ability to publicize cruelty and injustice is feared by those guilty of abusing human rights.

Broader Campaigns

Amnesty International now also runs campaigns on general human rights issues, including discrimination against women and people who are gay. It has also taken up the cause of children, particularly child prisoners and children forced to fight in armed forces.

▲ *Amnesty International has highlighted the fate of women such as Katia Bengana, killed by Islamic armed groups in Algeria because she refused to wear a veil.*

Problem

Amnesty International first developed in Western Europe and North America. When it began to criticize abuses in countries in Asia, Africa, and South America, some people accused it of trying to impose the values of the "white" West on poorer countries, many of which had until recently been ruled by Europeans as colonies. They said human rights were a luxury that Western Europe and North America could afford, but that poor developing countries could not. However, Amnesty International has always insisted on the same human rights standard for all countries. It has gained members in every continent around the world.

▲ *Amnesty International members in Ukraine collect signatures for a petition on human rights.*

3. Amnesty International at Work

Amnesty International is structured to make sure that the work of over a million volunteers worldwide is as effective as possible.

International Council

More than 55 countries have national Amnesty International "sections." These are national offices that coordinate the work of local volunteer groups. Every two years, the members of these national sections elect representatives to an International Council, a kind of parliament that decides what policies Amnesty International should follow. The International Council then elects an International Executive Committee to carry out these policies.

◀ *Pierre Sané, secretary-general of Amnesty International, is the head of the International Secretariat — the permanent staff of professionals at the core of the organization.*

Checklist

Amnesty International:

- has more than one million members
- has members in over 140 countries
- has sections in 55 countries
- has over 7,500 volunteer local groups, youth, student, and other specialist groups
- works on behalf of some 5,000 prisoners every year
- has brought attention to 45,000 individual cases since 1961.

▲ *An Amnesty International volunteer in Lahore, Pakistan, signs up a new member.*

International Secretariat

The central office of Amnesty International is the International Secretariat in London. Here, researchers investigate allegations of human rights abuses and prepare reports on individual countries. The International Secretariat sends representatives to talk to national governments about their treatment of prisoners. It also sends people to observe trials and report on their fairness. The Secretariat organizes campaigns targeted at particular countries. For example, in October 1998, Amnesty International launched a campaign against human rights violations in the United States, including the death penalty, shackling of pregnant women prisoners, and mistreatment of children in prison. The International Secretariat also runs campaigns on specific issues. For example, it has put pressure on governments not to sell arms to countries that might use them against unarmed protesters.

▼ *An Amnesty International protest in Norway against the execution of U.S. citizen Sean Sellers, for murders he committed when he was just 16.*

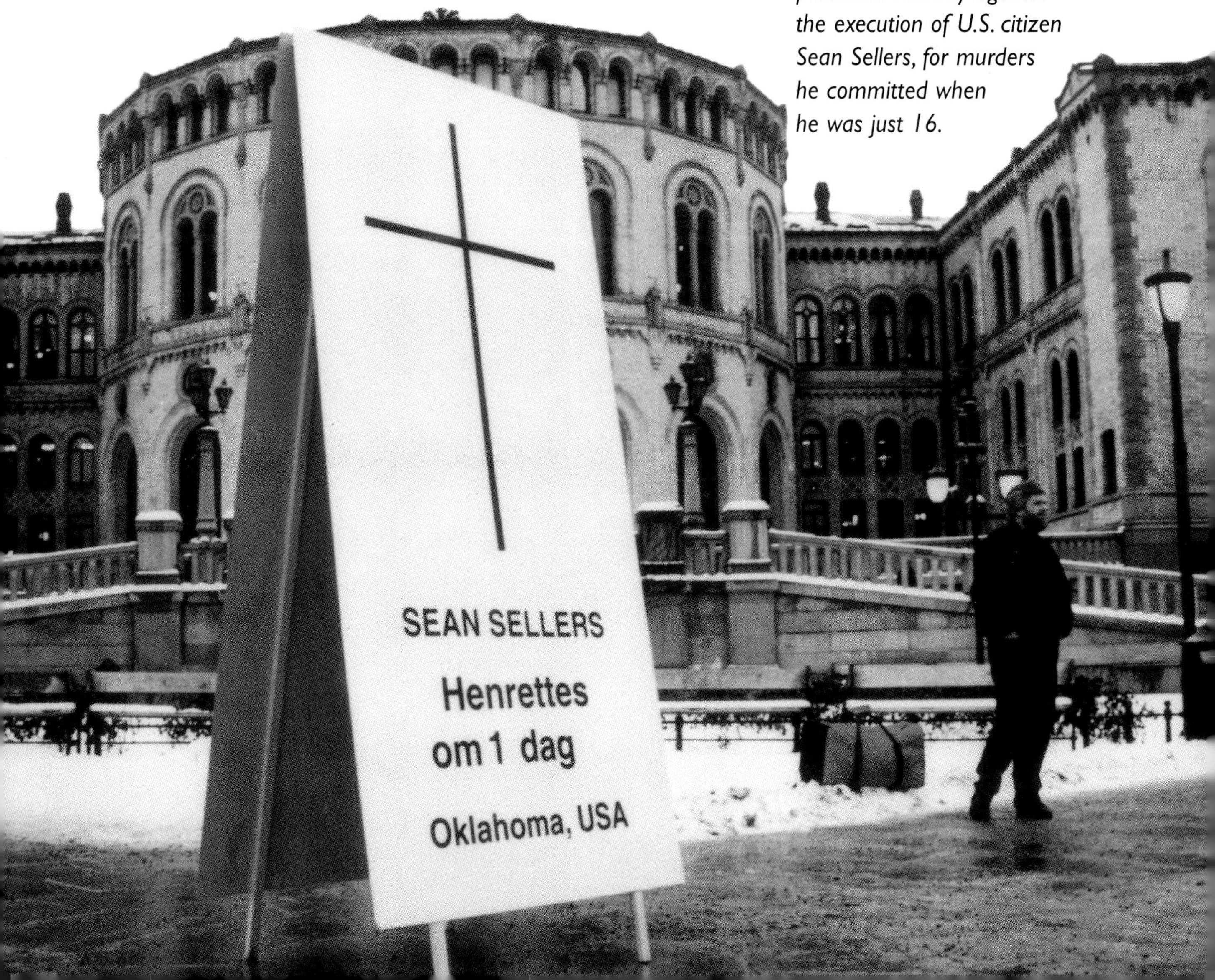

Vital Volunteers

Although its permanent staff is important, the key to Amnesty International's success is the painstaking work of local groups of unpaid volunteers. A group may be a circle of half a dozen friends who get together to write letters on behalf of Amnesty International. It may be 20 or 30 people who live in the same town or village. It may be a group of students or medical experts or members of a religious group.

Volunteers send letters, faxes, or e-mails to governments about the fate of individual prisoners of conscience. They try to interest their local newspapers and radio and television stations in Amnesty International cases. They lobby local politicians, trying to get them to support causes such as the abolition of the death penalty. They organize fund-raising events and demonstrations and attract new members by handing out informational leaflets and educational material.

▲ A poster advertises a fund-raising bicycle ride in Pakistan in 1995. It raised money for a human rights education institute.

▶ Musician Baaba Maal takes part in a concert to raise money for Amnesty International.

Specialist Volunteers

There are also international networks of specialist volunteers who work for Amnesty International in specific areas. They include doctors, who prepare reports on issues such as the use of injections as a way of executing prisoners, and lawyers, who bring their expertise to bear on human rights issues.

Spotlight

Amnesty International organized a worldwide campaign on the 50th anniversary of the UN Universal Declaration of Human Rights in 1998. Using the slogan "Get Up! Sign Up!" activists collected 13 million signatures in support of the declaration from people in more than 120 countries. Signers pledged to do all they could to make sure that human rights "become a reality around the world." A book containing over a million of the signatures was presented to the UN Secretary-General Kofi Annan at a special ceremony.

▸ *Amnesty International's Pierre Sané hands a book containing a million human rights pledges to UN Secretary-General Kofi Annan in December 1998.*

4. Prisoners of Conscience

The core of Amnesty International's work has always been its demand for the release of prisoners of conscience.

Reasons for Arrest

The prisoners of conscience may be people who have spoken out against their country's government. They may belong to an opposition political party, or they may be related to someone in an opposition party. They may be a member of a religious group against the regime. They may have refused to do military service.

Non-violence

A person arrested for any of these reasons can be adopted by Amnesty International as a prisoner of conscience, providing they have never used violence or encouraged other people to use violence. Amnesty International researchers will then begin a careful investigation of the case to ensure that the facts are clear. When research has established solid evidence that a person has been arrested because of their beliefs or simply because of who they are, and that they have never used or advocated violence, Amnesty International adopts them as a prisoner of conscience.

Pressure for Release

The case is then given to a number of volunteer groups. They learn all they can about the case and then begin writing letters to the people responsible for the prisoner's confinement, demanding his or her immediate release. They may also contact the prisoner's family or write to the prisoner expressing support. They will publicize the case as widely as they can and try to get famous people to lend their support.

Volunteer groups never work on cases in their own country. This helps them to be objective about the case and protects them from reprisals from the government or police.

▲ *Tibetan monk Palden Gyalso shows the damage to his mouth caused by torture instruments. He was held prisoner by the Chinese for 33 years after taking part in Tibetan resistance to Chinese rule.*

▲ *Children in Taiwan sign Amnesty International appeals on behalf of prisoners of conscience around the world. Such appeals have often proved effective in winning a prisoner release or better treatment.*

Spotlight

Christina Anyanwu is a Nigerian journalist. In 1995 she was arrested for writing an article the government did not like and was sentenced to life imprisonment. Amnesty International adopted her as a prisoner of conscience. One day, prison guards brought in sack after sack of mail for her. Inside were 11,000 letters and cards from Amnesty International and other organizations expressing support for her. She pasted the cards on the wall of her cell. "I gained such strength from them," she later said. "I knew I had committed no crime and now I knew that the world also knew..." Anyanwu was eventually released from prison in 1998. She thanked the volunteers who had written to her. "Others have not been as lucky as me," she said. "I was lucky – I had you."

Spotlight

Amnesty International never expresses an opinion about the political situation that is the background to a prisoner of conscience case. Amnesty International does not work to change the political system in the country where the prisoner is being held, or say that the prisoner is right to criticize the government. It simply demands the immediate release of prisoners of conscience and good treatment for all prisoners.

▲ *Children from Myanmar (Burma) hold up pictures of pro-democracy campaigner Aung San Suu Kyi. She has effectively been put under house arrest by the country's military government since 1989.*

Spotlight

In Somalia in 1985, Safia Hashi Madar was dragged from her home by police in the middle of the night and thrown into prison. She never knew exactly why she had been arrested. She was pregnant at the time, and gave birth three days after her arrest. Her baby was immediately taken away from her. She was kept in a dark cell with only the floor to sleep on, and was tortured — kicked, beaten, and burned with cigarettes.

Safia was adopted as an Amnesty International prisoner of conscience, and three volunteer groups wrote hundreds of letters and postcards to the Somali government on her behalf. When she fell ill in prison, Amnesty International launched an Urgent Action on her behalf. After thousands of letters were sent to the Somali Ministry of Health, Safia eventually received medical treatment that saved her life. She was finally released in 1989.

Urgent Action

When Amnesty International learns that a prisoner is facing torture, execution, or death from bad health, it organizes an Urgent Action. Volunteers are asked to send a flood of faxes, e-mails, and letters to the relevant authorities. Amnesty International contacts the government to demand instant action to stop the mistreatment. On average, this pressure results in improvement in about one case in three.

▲ *Pierre Sané holds up an Amnesty International Urgent Action appeal in front of a map of East Timor — the site of many serious human rights abuses by the Indonesian government.*

▸ *A Japanese group demonstrates to draw attention to a prisoner of conscience they have adopted, María Elena Aparicio, in Cuba.*

Giving Hope

Amnesty International never claims full credit for the release of prisoners. Releases are the result of many factors — often, for example, the families of the prisoner play a large role. But many released prisoners have expressed their gratitude to Amnesty International. Many have described how conditions in prison improved once Amnesty International took up their case, how torture stopped, or how food or medical care improved. Above all, they were given hope — they knew they had not been forgotten.

▼ Nelson Mandela once called for an armed uprising against the apartheid regime. This made him unsuitable as an Amnesty International prisoner of conscience.

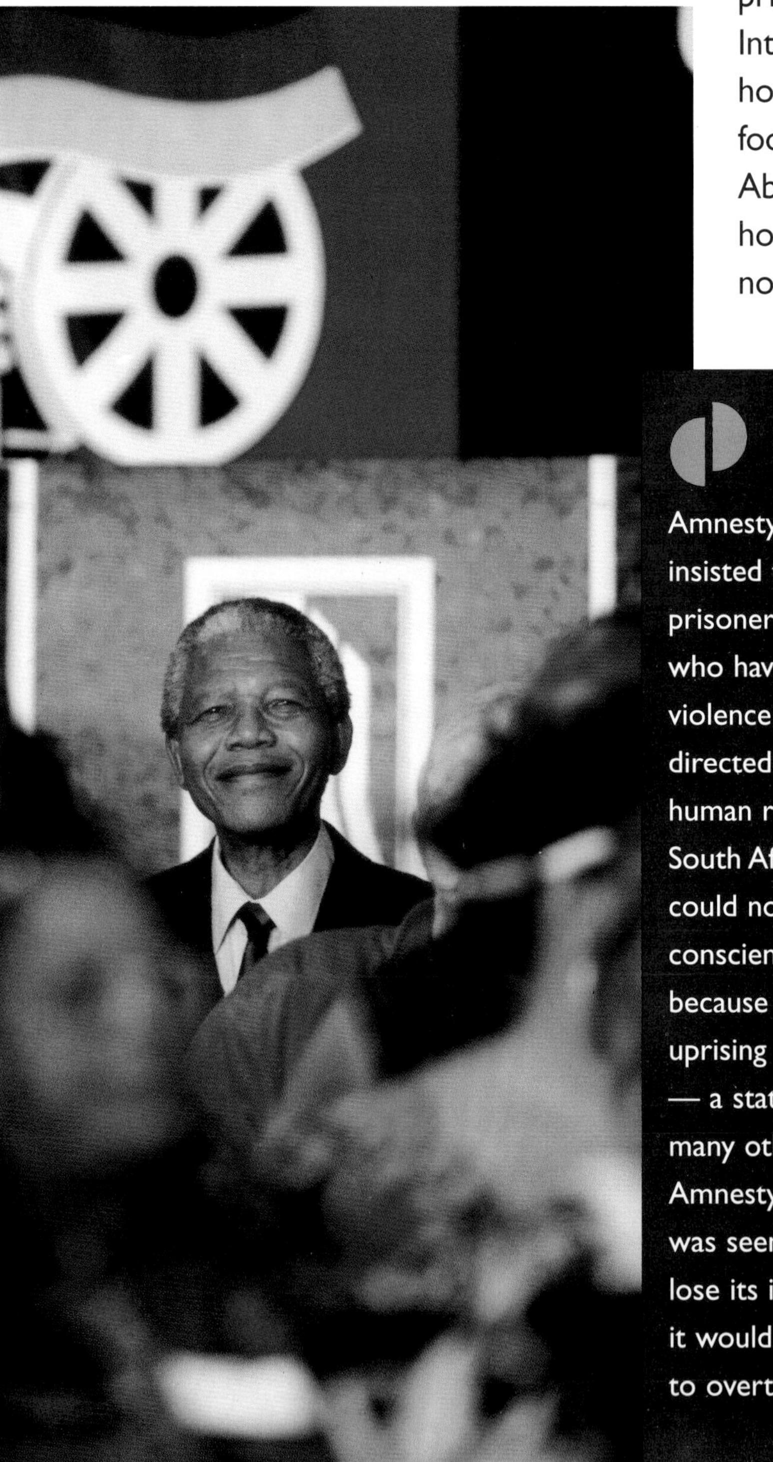

Problem

Amnesty International has always insisted that it cannot adopt as prisoners of conscience people who have used violence or advocated violence, even when the violence is directed against states that abuse human rights. For example, the future South African President Nelson Mandela could not be adopted as a prisoner of conscience during his 27 years in jail because he had backed an armed uprising against white-ruled South Africa — a state that was guilty of torture and many other crimes against humanity. Amnesty International insists that if it was seen to support violence, it would lose its influence. Some people feel that it would be better to support attempts to overthrow evil regimes.

5. Children in Danger

Children are among the worst sufferers from cruelty and injustice. Across the world, millions of children live in extreme poverty or are forced to work long hours every day for virtually no pay. Amnesty International takes a special interest in the fate of children who become prisoners or refugees, or who are forced to fight as soldiers.

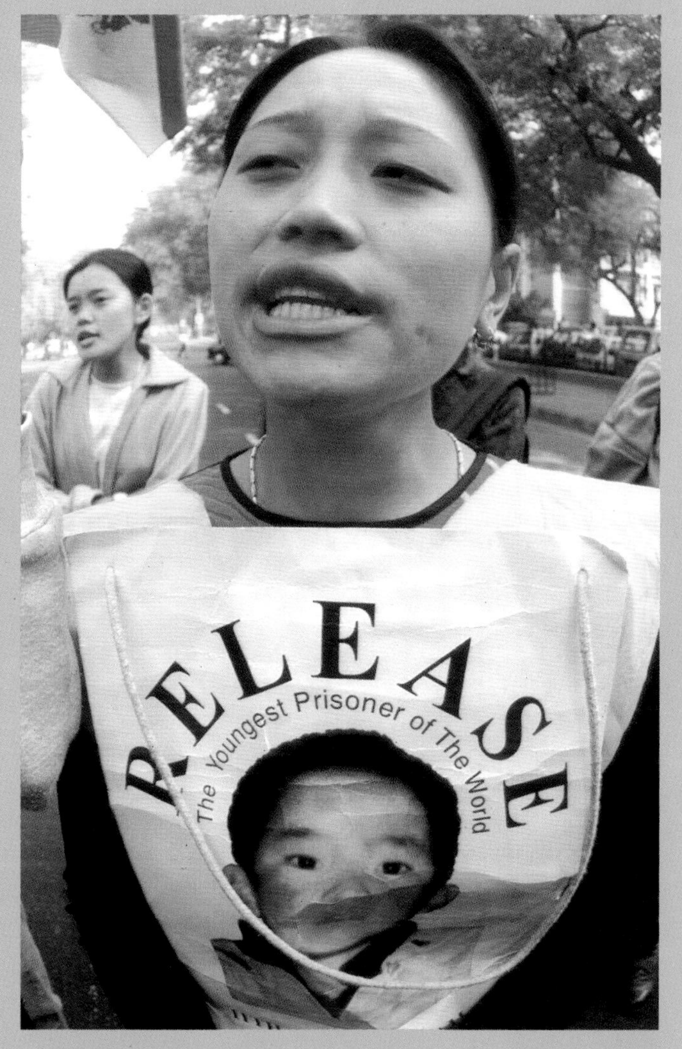

▲ *Tibet's Panchen Lama has been called "the youngest prisoner of the world," since he was allegedly abducted by the Chinese authorities in 1995 at the age of six.*

▲ *Homeless children in many parts of the world are often rounded up and put in jail.*

Children in Prison

Many children worldwide are put in prison for minor crimes often linked to poverty. Children who live on the streets may be arrested for vagrancy — the crime of having no home — or for petty theft. Some children are arrested for political reasons — either because of their parents' political activities or just because they belong to the wrong ethnic or religious group.

In prison, children are often kept in overcrowded cells with poor food and sanitation. They may be held with adult prisoners instead of being held separately. Amnesty International campaigns for proper treatment for all child prisoners.

Death and Disappearance

Children also feature in Amnesty International's campaigns against the death penalty and "disappearances." For example, in the United States, individuals have been sentenced to death for crimes they committed when they were under 18.

Spotlight

In 1990 Amnesty International reported that hundreds of children living on the streets of cities in Brazil were being murdered every year. The killings were carried out by death squads organized by the Brazilian police. There were estimated to be seven million street children in Brazil. Some people in authority had decided that these children were a nuisance and should be disposed of. The Amnesty International report led to widespread protests. The Brazilian government eventually stepped in to crack down on the activities of the death squads.

▼ *Brazilian street children went to parliament in 1999 to protest moves to lower the age at which children can be held responsible for crimes.*

Child soldiers, armed to the teeth, fight in the civil war in Liberia, West Africa.

Problem

Amnesty International supports demands for a ban on young people under the age of 18 joining the armed forces. But governments in many countries, including the United States and the United Kingdom, think that it is alright to recruit soldiers or sailors at the age of 16 or 17, because by then they are no longer children.

▲ *This child is a refugee who fled from his home in Rwanda in 1994 to avoid brutal massacres.*

Soldiers and Refugees

Amnesty International has joined with other NGOs to try to stop the use of children as soldiers in wars. There may be as many as 300,000 children fighting in wars around the world today. As well as facing death or injury in fighting, they often suffer from brutal treatment at the hands of adult soldiers. They are often damaged psychologically by seeing people being killed or tortured, or even by taking part in atrocities. In 1997, children under 15 were engaged in warfare in 24 countries, including Afghanistan, Angola, Cambodia, Colombia, Myanmar (Burma), and Sierra Leone.

Amnesty International estimates that more than half the world's refugees are children, about 20 million in all. It campaigns for authorities to recognize the special needs of refugee children, especially those who have been separated from their parents.

A group of Argentinian children take part in an event designed to teach them the meaning of human rights.

Human Rights Education

Amnesty International believes all children need to be educated in human rights so that the next generation of adults will stand up for their own rights and for the rights of their fellow citizens. Amnesty International has put pressure on governments to make human rights education a part of every child's schooling. It has provided courses for teachers and has also produced books and other school materials. In the end, the hope for a better future lies in the hands of today's children.

Spotlight

Iqbal Masih (below) was born in Pakistan. At the age of four, his parents sold him to the owner of a carpet factory. He worked in the factory for six years, chained to a carpet weaving loom. His experience made him lead a campaign against child labor, which was so successful that he became famous. But in 1995, at the age of 12, he was shot dead. Factory owners are suspected of having ordered him killed.

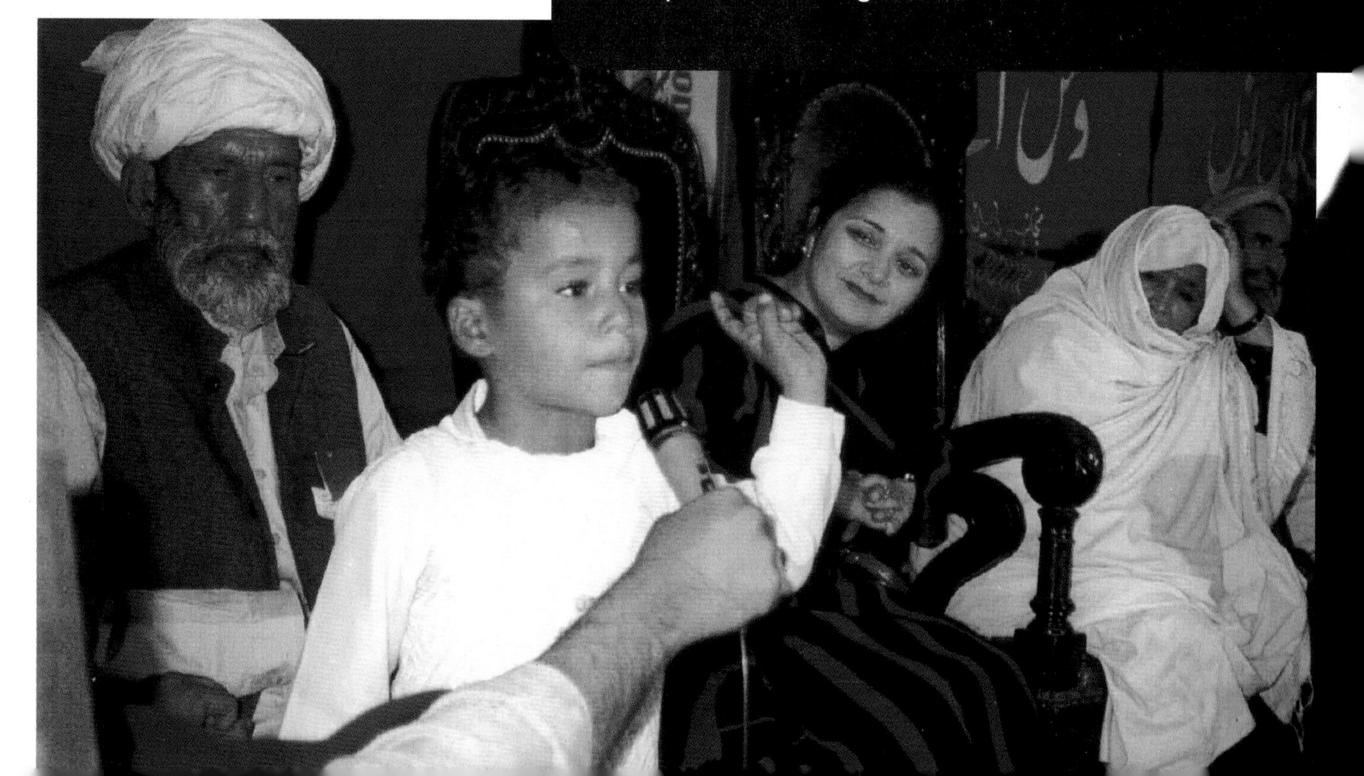

6. Keeping Watch

These women and children from the Hutu ethnic group in Burundi have witnessed atrocities and fear that more may happen in the future.

Amnesty International aims to help create a world in which there are no prisoners of conscience and no torture, and where human rights are universally respected. But after Amnesty International had been in existence for almost 40 years, there was no sign of this aim being achieved.

The Killing Goes On

In the 1990s, the world witnessed disasters such as massacres in Rwanda and mass killings in the former Yugoslavia. From China to Colombia, from Algeria to Indonesia, from Iraq to Myanmar (Burma), millions of people were victims of wrongful imprisonment, torture and politically motivated killing.

19-year-old Vlora Maliqi was badly beaten by Serbian police after taking part in a peaceful demonstration in Kosovo in 1998.

Checklist

According to Amnesty International, in 1998 there were:

- prisoners of conscience in 78 countries
- torture or ill treatment of prisoners in 125 countries
- unfair trials in 35 countries
- arrest without charge or trial in 66 countries
- more than 1,625 prisoners executed in 36 countries
- extrajudicial murders in 47 countries
- "disappeared" people in 37 countries
- crimes by armed opposition groups in 37 countries.

Stopping the Death Penalty

Amnesty International activists were encouraged, however, by signs that governments were paying increasing attention to human rights. The abolition of the death penalty was one example of progress in human rights. When the United Nation's Universal Declaration of Human Rights was adopted in 1948, only eight countries had abolished the death penalty. By 1999, 67 countries had done so.

Human Rights

Amnesty International also supported moves to bring people responsible for crimes against humanity to court. In the 1990s, two international courts were set up to try people for such crimes. These were the International Criminal Tribunal for Rwanda and the International Criminal Tribunal for the Former Yugoslavia. Amnesty International was also active in support of plans to set up a permanent International Criminal Court.

Amnesty International lobbies governments and businesses to always take human rights into account. For example, it pressured governments not to sell arms to countries that were using them to suppress freedom of speech or carry out massacres.

▼ *South Korean women hold up pictures of relatives who are held in prison for opposing the government. Some of them have been prisoners for decades.*

A Shining Light

Amnesty International continues to be a thorn in the side of any government or organization that locks people up for their beliefs, uses torture, or tries to make its opponents "disappear." Such crimes against humanity flourish in secrecy and silence. Amnesty International tries to shine a light into these dark places and ensure that the sufferings of the victims of oppression are known to the world.

Spotlight

In 1999, Amnesty International ran a campaign against human rights abuses in China. It was timed for the tenth anniversary of the Tiananmen Square massacre, when demonstrations in favor of democracy were brutally put down by the Chinese authorities. Amnesty International collected 150,000 signatures for a petition asking the Chinese government to release prisoners of conscience.

Spotlight

The effort to prosecute people for crimes against humanity was highlighted by the case of the former president of Chile, General Augusto Pinochet (below). In 1998, Pinochet was arrested while visiting Britain for medical treatment. The British authorities had been asked by a Spanish magistrate to hand over Pinochet to them for trial on charges of murder and torture. Many thousands of people were killed and tortured after Pinochet took power in Chile in 1973, including Spanish citizens. Amnesty International supported the move to try Pinochet, claiming that it would deter other rulers from ignoring human rights.

Glossary

amnesty a general pardon for prisoners.

armistice truce, especially a permanent truce. The word comes from the Latin *arma* (arms) and *sisto* (make stand).

atrocities extremely cruel, brutal acts, especially against defenseless people.

capital punishment punishment by death.

CIA the Central Intelligence Agency, an organization set up by the American government to carry out spying and other secret activities, chiefly against communists in other countries.

Cold War the armed confrontation between the United States and its allies on one side and the communist Soviet Union and its allies on the other. It lasted from the late 1940s to the 1980s.

colony a country ruled by a foreign power as part of its empire.

communism a political and economic system first established in the Soviet Union after a revolution in 1917 and then spread to many other countries; typically, it involved rule by a single political party that allowed no opposition, and control of industry and agriculture by the state.

crimes against humanity acts such as torture and mass killing that may be treated as crimes by the international community.

democracy political system in which people elect their rulers.

discrimination unfavorable treatment of a person or group, for example because of their race (racial discrimination) or their sex (sexual discrimination).

dissidents the term used for opponents of oppressive governments, especially opponents of the communist regimes in the Soviet Union and eastern Europe.

extrajudicial murder the killing of prisoners without a trial or other legal process.

freedom of expression the right to say or write what you believe to be the truth.

guerrillas lightly armed fighters usually engaged in a war against the government of their own country or an invader.

human rights freedoms that all humans should have the right to enjoy, wherever they live and whatever their government.

human rights abuses actions that deny individuals or groups their fundamental human rights.

lobby to put pressure on politicians or governments, especially by talking or writing to them.

military coup seizure of power by the armed forces of a country.

NGO a Non-Governmental Organization — for example, Amnesty International.

Useful Addresses

Panchen Lama a spiritual leader of Tibetan Buddhism, second only in importance to the Dalai Lama.

petition a document signed by a large number of people calling on a government or governments to take a particular course of action or remedy an abuse.

political prisoners people held in prison as a result of illegal actions they have carried out in opposition to their government.

prisoners of conscience people held in prison for exercising their human rights, such as the right to freedom of expression, or because of the ethnic or religious group to which they belong.

security of person the right to be free of arrest or imprisonment unless charged with a specific crime and properly tried before a court.

shackling the use of handcuffs, chains, and other devices to limit a prisoner's movements.

Soviet Union the communist state that until 1991 ruled a vast area of Europe and Asia, including Russia, Ukraine, Belarus, Georgia, Armenia, and Kazakhstan.

street children children who have no homes and live on the streets.

volunteer a person who works without being paid or forced to do so.

Amnesty International Secretariat
1 Easton Street, London WC1X 8DJ

Amnesty International U.S.A. Regional Offices
- Northeast Region: 58 Day Street, Davis Square, Somerville, MA 02114
- Southern Region: 131 Ponce de Leon Ave, NE, 220, Atlanta, GA 30308
- Midwest Region: 53 W. Jackson, Suite 731, Chicago, IL 60604
- Mid-Atlantic Region: 600 Penn Ave. SE 5th Floor, Washington, DC 20003
- Western Region: 9000 W. Washington Bl, 2nd Floor, Culver City, CA 90232 or 500 Sansome St, Suite 615, San Francisco, CA 94111

Useful Websites
- Amnesty International:
www.amnesty.org

- Human Rights Watch
www.hrw.org

- The Universal Declaration of Human Rights (in a wide range of languages):
www.egt.ie/udhr/udhr.html

Get Involved!

If you are between 8 and 12 years old, you can join Amnesty International's Junior Urgent Action network. Ask an adult to contact your national Amnesty International section for you. You will receive a monthly Junior Urgent Action telling you about an Amnesty International case, usually involving a child. If you want, you will be able to write letters on behalf of the victim.

If you are between 11 and 18 years old, you can form a Youth Group at your school or college. Amnesty International will send you information on how to campaign against human rights abuses through letter writing and other activities, and how to hold fund-raising events.

Index